How Is Chocolate Made?

by Grace Hansen

abdopublishing.com

Published by Abdo Kids, a division of ABDO, P.O. Box 398166, Minneapolis, Minnesota 55439.

Printed in the United States of America, North Mankato, Minnesota.

052017

092017

Photo Credits: Alamy, AP Images, iStock, Shutterstock

Production Contributors: Teddy Borth, Jennie Forsberg, Grace Hansen

Design Contributors: Dorothy Toth, Laura Mitchell

Publisher's Cataloging in Publication Data

Names: Hansen, Grace, author.

Title: How is chocolate made? / by Grace Hansen.

Description: Minneapolis, Minnesota : Abdo Kids, 2018 | Series: How is it made? | Includes bibliographical references and index.

Identifiers: LCCN 2016962398 | ISBN 9781532100451 (lib. bdg.) | ISBN 9781532101144 (ebook) | ISBN 9781532101694 (Read-to-me ebook)

Subjects: LCSH: Chocolate--Juvenile literature. | Chocolate processing--Juvenile literature.

Classification: DDC 664/.5--dc23

LC record available at http://lccn.loc.gov/2016962398

Table of Contents

Cacao Tree Farms

Most cacao beans are grown in Africa. They grow on cacao trees.

Africa

Cacao trees grow large **pods**. Inside the pods are 30 to 40 seeds. These seeds are called cacao beans.

The beans are a pale color. They are dried in the sun. This turns them brown. The beans are very **bitter**. They must go through a process that changes their flavor.

Chocolate Factory

The cacao beans are sent from farm to manufacturer. Here, they are roasted. Large ovens heat the beans to nearly 300 degrees F (149 °C). The beans roast for up to two hours.

After the beans are roasted, they must be **winnowed**. This process separates the shells from the **nibs**.

The **nibs** are ground into a paste. The paste is **bitter**. It does not taste very good!

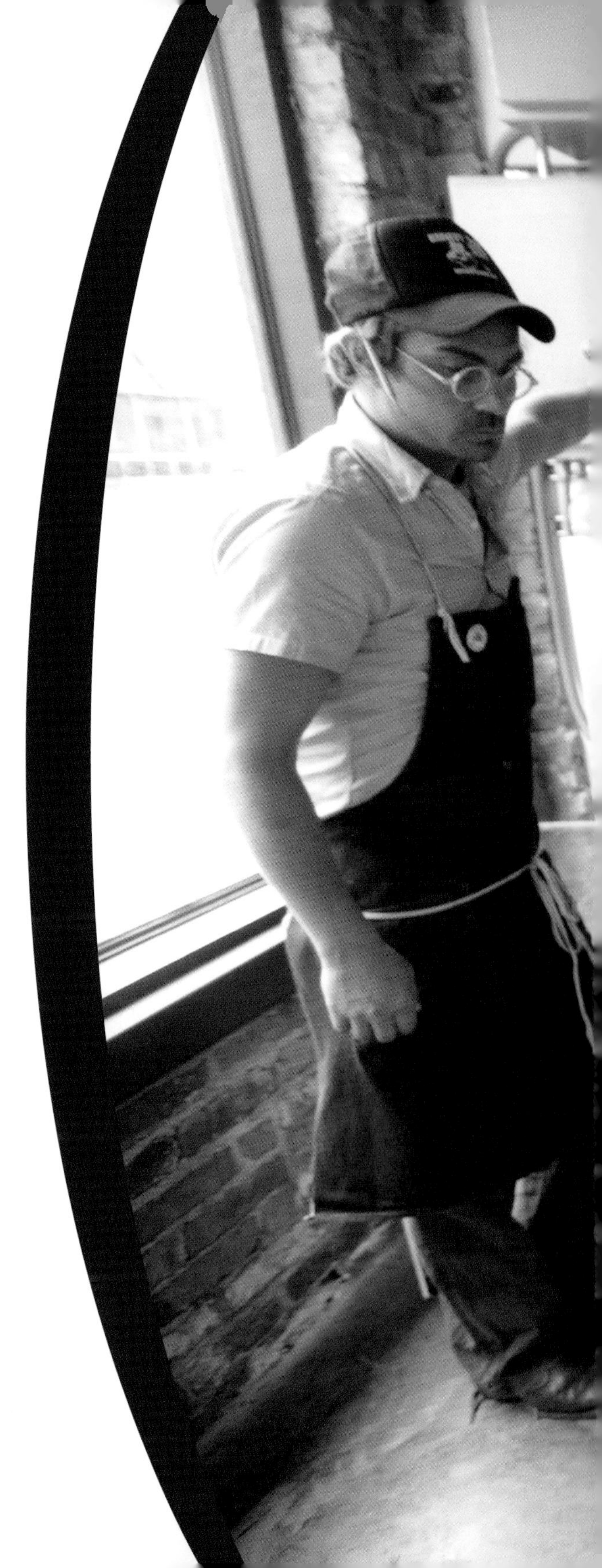

EAT

The manufacturer adds ingredients like sugar and vanilla. This sweetens the paste. Milk is added to make milk chocolate.

The sweet mixture is sent through rollers. This creates a smooth texture. It also brings out the flavors.

Ready to Ship!

The chocolate is heated and cooled several times. This makes it look shiny. It is now ready to be poured into molds. It is cooled, packaged, and shipped to stores!

More Facts

- It takes about 400 cacao beans to make 1 pound (0.5 kg) of chocolate.

- About 70% of cacao is grown in West Africa.

- A cacao tree must be 4 or 5 years old before it can grow its first beans.

Glossary

bitter - having a sharp, bad taste that is not sour or salty.

nib - chocolate in its purest form before anything else is added.

pod - grows from cacao trees and contains the beans that chocolate is made from.

winnow - to sift through and separate the needed parts from the unneeded parts.

Index

abdokids.com

Use this code to log on to abdokids.com and access crafts, games, videos and more!